I0486807

What Medical School Did Not Teach You

About Financial Planning

Chad Olivier, CFP®

Outskirts Press, Inc.
Denver, Colorado

What Medical School Did Not Teach You About Financial Planning

Outskirts Press, Inc.
http://www.outskirtspress.com

ISBN: 978-1-4327-0970-9

Outskirts Press and the "OP" logo are trademarks belonging to Outskirts Press, Inc.

PRINTED IN THE UNITED STATES OF AMERICA

Library of Congress Control Number: 2007937513

To Rose, and our boys Conrad and Cole – the inspiration and love of my life.

Foreword

"Try not to become a man of success but rather try to become a man of value."

Albert Einstein

Medical school education demands perfection in the sciences. Unfortunately, it does not offer money management courses, nor does the student have time to seek financial knowledge. I am not referring to merely balancing a check book; I mean investment strategies and portfolio options with the goal of "money making money." In addition, the physician's limited time outside of his practice is either devoted to his family or consumed by continued medical education. A physician can walk into the doctors' lounge and obtain a feeling of how the DOW is doing. A lot of talking, the DOW is doing great! Little to no talking, the DOW is down. The point being that there are important issues in our daily life that require guidance. Solid financial advice is paramount among these issues.

As I evaluated various companies regarding my financial future, one quality was at the top of my list: character. How can I trust my financial future with this company or individual? As I discussed my financial values with the prospective advisor, I asked about his family. I observed the *manner* in which the person responded to the question. I was not as concerned with the answer, but *how* it was answered. Was this advisor committed to the same values that I uphold? If yes, I further inquired about other non-financial situations. If not, my decision was easy. Chad's overall values of family, commitment, respect, and integrity were straightforwardly quantified as solid. He is the type of individual that one would desire to have in the fox hole.

These qualities were complemented by his extensive knowledge of financial situations and market analysis. Deciding to have Chad direct my financial investment portfolio was uncomplicated; I trust him. He is energetic and committed to my family's financial future. I do not agonize about my financial success; it is as solid as my financial advisor. However, I continue to converse in the physicians' lounge.

Cullen Hebert, M.D., FACP, FCCP
Pulmonary/Critical Care

Contents

School's Out, Now What?

In general, it is known that as a physician or other medical professional, you have one of the nation's most stressful jobs, regardless of whether you are a veteran to the field or a new graduate. The stress, in addition to a lack of free time, could potentially cause you to neglect any type of financial planning efforts.

The good (and bad) news is that you are the ideal consumer for whom financial institutions spend large amounts of marketing dollars to influence. Banks salivate over the potential loan and investment revenue that will come their way as a result of your earning potential. The insurance industry is well aware of the liability premiums medical professionals are made to pay and the different insurance products that will be marketed to you and your peers.

This book is written to help steer you in a

direction of balance sheet wealth, as opposed to financial statement wealth. It will provide information that is valuable to both new and experienced physicians. I will breakdown the complex jargon associated with the planning process into simple terms to teach you how to manage your wealth and create a functional and maintainable financial plan.

Initially taking you through the planning process, the first chapter outlines how to approach financial planning as a whole and the advisors that should be able to help with your efforts. Remember, the goal of actual planning is to set a plan in place, then *implement* it. It is too late to try and implement after the fact. A person who gets in a car accident and tells their insurance agent the following day to increase coverage is too late; the old coverage would stand, potentially putting their assets at risk. This is an example of having a plan, but waiting to implement it.

I will answer how much and what kind of insurance is necessary, so you can not only properly plan for catastrophic or unusual events, but also set those formed plans in place. Once you are protected, then you can sit back and know you are prepared for the "just in case" scenarios.

After going through the in and outs of loans, borrowing, and insurance, the book will proceed to delve into investing. I use a pyramid chart to illustrate different investments and how they fit into your financial parameters. The pyramid chart also gives details about how diversified portfolios perform under certain conditions and the underused yet highly important 'Investment Policy Statement,' which could dictate portfolio allocation.

Following the investing section, I discuss retirement planning. This is where different plans and their corresponding benefits are explained. The earlier you begin planning for your retirement, the less hassle you will encounter in the future.

The last section is high-end planning. This explains how to turn financial planning into achieving specific attainable goals, such as passing your estate to beneficiaries the most tax-efficient way possible. The techniques discussed in this section will enhance your financial security and move your estate in a smooth, proficient manner. I will conclude by offering advice on how to find the right advisor for you.

Planning your finances can prove to be a daunting task for one individual. Knowing the basics of each financial area can help you lay a solid foundation on which to build upon as your career grows. School may be out, but now is the time to start learning what may not have been covered in class, how to create a solid financial future.

Chapter 1

Financial Planning

What is Financial Planning and Why is it Important?

Financial planning is an all-encompassing approach to managing and allocating finances. It is devising a strategy that puts together all aspects of your personal and business planning. An effective financial plan manages your current and future assets, debts, and liability coverage, as well as positions those assets in the most tax-efficient manner. We will examine this topic in more detail later in the chapter.

The next question might be: Why is financial planning so important? I know you have heard the saying "the rich get richer and poor get poorer." There is an underlying meaning to this saying: wealthy individuals understand how to generate and maintain money while the poor do not. One thing those who have maintained their wealth have in common is that they are smart enough to hire high quality professionals to protect their wealth. Did you notice I said protect their wealth and not increase their wealth? Physicians grow their wealth by practicing medicine, the skill-set they learned in medical school. Perception of money is what will set people apart in the financial world.

The high-income producer's biggest concern should be protecting what he is earning. Let's look at a basic example:

$40,000 put in savings each year
25 years
0% growth rate
Value in 25 years = **$1,000,000**

$40,000 put in savings each year
25 years
5% growth rate
Value in 25 years = **$1,909,088**
These are hypothetical illustrations and are not representative of any investment.

Of course, you may have heard the argument of trying to get the highest returns possible to have a nice early retirement. The problem with this argument is that with higher returns comes the increased probability of losses. Be aware! The way to avoid these pitfalls is to be prepared and educated.

The following is an article I wrote explaining the theory of lower volatility giving higher returns that challenges the aforementioned argument.

"The Volatility Factor:
Can less volatility and lower returns equal more money?"

Lower returns can equal more money. At first glance, this statement may appear contradictory and unfeasible, but do not allow yourself to be fooled. I can hear the questions in your head: "What is he talking about?" "How can that be possible?" Believe it or not, lower returns can possibly have a positive effect on your portfolio.

Throughout the 90s, we witnessed the emergence of the technology / internet boom. We all heard the stories of the new "Generation X" kids making millions by starting their own internet company and bringing it public. Due to this quickly developed trend, the day-traders and the new technology mutual funds emerged, all trying to capitalize on the emotions of the time. Many people dove into the market after receiving hot stock tips, which were supposed to lead them directly to wealth. As a result of those conditions, many investors resisted remaining in a proper asset-allocation strategy. (Asset Allocation is the process of distributing assets throughout different asset classes and categories while diversifying, and in turn, lowering volatility and risk in the portfolio). We all know what happened in the years 2000 – 2002. The "Bubble Burst" left many people holding worthless or depressed investments.

Now, let us fast forward to 2006. The following is an example of how volatility of returns affects your investment portfolio.

We have in one corner "Fast Eddie" who likes his cars and portfolio high-speed and in the fast lane. Fast Eddie wants big returns and is always eager and ready for the next big stock tip. Then, in the other corner, we have "Steady Rose" who realizes she has worked very hard for her money and would like it to consistently grow without big fluctuations. Let us take a look at their portfolios to see how market volatility affects each: (For purposes of this example, assume each invested $100,000 in 1998.)

	FAST EDDIE ($100,000)		**STEADY ROSE** ($100,000)	
Year	*Return*	*Investment*	*Return*	*Investment*
1998 /	60 %	$160,000	8%	$108,000
1999 /	40%	$224,000	7%	$115,560
2000 /	-40%	$134,400	-2%	$113,248
2001 /	-15%	$114,240	0%	$113,248
2002 /	-10%	$102,816	2%	$115,513
2003 /	15%	$118,238	6%	$122,444
2004 /	10%	$130,062	6%	$129,791
2005 /	5%	**$136,565.40**	7%	**$138,876**

Average
Return: **8.125%**   **4.25%**

This is a hypothetical example and is not representative of any specific situation. Your results will vary.

By calculating the average annual returns over the 7 year period from 1998 to 2005, Fast Eddie had an 8.125% average annual return, while Steady Rose only had a 4.25% average annual return. However, as you can see, Steady Rose's ending value was higher than Fast Eddie's which is attributable to lower volatility. A lower volatility portfolio could equal higher investment values.

This article tells us to pursue the consistent returns, not getting caught in the "Fast Eddie" mindset of constantly going for the homerun. Once you acquire big negative losses in a portfolio, it may take years to break even.

Not quite convinced? Let us look at another example:

Doctor Example's Investment Portfolio:
$1 million
Has a loss of 30%
Value = $700,000

- It will take over 9 years to get back to the $1 million at an 8% annualized return.

- It will take over 10 years to get back to the $1 million at a 7% annualized return.

This is only for Doctor Example to break even without considering his potential earnings if he had never made the bad investment choices that gave him a 30% loss.

What if the Doctor never made the bad investments and consistently yielded 5% for the 9 years after the portfolio attained $1 million? The result would be a portfolio of $1,551,328.

Remember, these examples are hypothetical and are not representative of any specific investment.

Difference between Advice and Selling

The Insurance Industry

There is no single financial product that has the ability to meet all of your financial planning needs. To develop a truly effective plan, you will need different investment products and insurance vehicles. Be aware when you are approached by your insurance agent for investments and insurance products. In most cases, the more complicated the product, the more commissions your agent makes. I am not saying that these are necessarily bad products, but if you are approached by an agent, he may try to fit his one product into all aspects of your situation.

Rule number one: An investment or insurance product should not be sold to you on the first meeting.

Rule number two: If you are meeting with an insurance agent who represents only one company, ask yourself, "Is a single company going to be adequate for my financial needs?"

Rule number three: Ok, let us stop here; we do not need any more rules in dealing with insurance agents. What you really need to know is that he or she is probably not where you want to start your planning process.

Say no to the insurance agent.

The Bank

The bank is where the money is and the bank wants to keep it that way. In most cases, the bank is bad for your financial portfolio. If you are putting money into CDs, borrowing money, and using the bank's checking services, the bank is a great institution to utilize. However, for your investing and insurance needs, it is best not to look to the bank. In many cases, you are dealing with bank brokers that have a narrow product selection and limited knowledge of investments and insurance products. Of course, all generalities come with exceptions; however, for most, the bank is not where you want to get your financial planning advice or investment products.

The Big Brokerage Firms

Be aware when dealing with the big brokerage firms. The good news about most of these big firms is that many of the financial advisors do have knowledge of investments. However, the bad news is that many firms require their representatives to produce more and more commission each year simply to hang on to their jobs. Producing greater commissions requires brokers to obtain more clients, meaning old clients get less attention. So, the question remains as to how they have time to handle your account and your needs while under constant pressure to obtain new clients. Are you being neglected? Often, the answer is yes. Take a look at this press release from the Paladin Registry, an independent source for finding financial professionals and firms:

"Financial Advisors from Brand Name Companies - Are They the Safest Choice for Investors?"

ROSEVILLE, California, August 2, 2006 -- Paladin Registry, LLC (www.paladinregistry.com) released additional results of a recent survey that showed more than 90% of investors did not know the right questions to ask to determine the quality of financial planners and advisors. The question is if they do not know how to determine advisor quality, then how do they select financial professionals?

Jack Waymire, Paladin founder and author of *Who's Watching Your Money?* said "Millions of investors use very subjective processes. One frequent method is to select advisors because they have likeable personalities and say the right things (sales pitches). Another popular, but equally subjective method, is selecting advisors from brand name financial services companies because they feel safer. However, are they really safer or is that a false sense of security that has been created

9

by billions of dollars of advertising?"

Advisors from brand name companies may not be the safe choice investors think they are for the following reasons:

- Their companies are publicly owned, so their first responsibility is to shareholders and not investors.

- In their companies' quests for profits and higher share prices, the advisors have more conflicts of interest than other financial professionals.

Waymire added, "If these facts aren't enough to raise concerns, then another telling statistic is the thousands of advisors who left brand name companies so they could do what was best for their clients. These advisors got fed-up with the constant pressure to sell products that maximized profits versus provide quality services that helped their clients achieve their goals. They couldn't change the system so they left."

Waymire also said, "Most of these breakaway advisors started their own Registered Investment Advisory firms or became Investment Advisor Representatives. For the first time, they were able to acknowledge their fiduciary status, work for fees, and they no longer had to cater to the demands of management to sell particular products regardless of quality. As independent professionals they had the freedom, flexibility, and choices to do what was best for their clients."

Advice

The burning question you are probably asking is: With so many places to seek advice, where is the *right* place to get advice? My answer is to research and choose an independent CERTIFIED FINANCIAL PLANNER™ practitioner to work with. Then, follow through with three steps:

1. Have them complete a comprehensive financial plan.
2. Meet with them to discuss your situation.
3. Make sure the person fits with you and your goals.

You can find a comprehensive list of CFPs by going to the website www.cfp.net or asking friends who they use and why. Remember, your CFP is like the quarterback of your financial team who is willing and able to assist you in all aspects of your financial life.

Good and Bad Habits

Saving for a house, new car, or even that great new motorboat you saw for sale requires that you have funds for the purchase. Perhaps you are great with your money and you have a savings account. We all wish we had good spending habits, so that we can afford bigger things in life. Unfortunately, we all have good and bad spending habits. This is why there are so many books about how to transform your habits into good ones. My two favorite and highly recommended books are both by the same author, Thomas Stanley: *The Millionaire Next Door* and *The Millionaire Mind*. These books explain the thought process of the balance-sheet millionaire as compared to the income statement millionaire and gives specific examples of the good and bad habits of each.

Good Habits

The difference between the two is the balance- sheet millionaires are the ones who have a budget and acquire large amounts of wealth while the income statement millionaire only appears to have the balance sheet to support his big house, fancy cars, and luxurious lifestyle. The truly affluent one is the balance-sheet millionaire. I have worked with a typical balance-sheet millionaire for several years now. His name is Glenny.

Let's take a look at Glenny's situation. I started helping Glenny manage his wealth back in 1999. Right away, I was very impressed with his financial thinking. We began by developing a detailed financial plan with over half of his assets in fixed income investments. This was in the roaring 90s when the stock market was giving high double-digit returns. Glenny was very level headed and knew he should always stay in a proper allocation, which consisted of over 50% of his portfolio in fixed income investments. One of the hardest aspects in my business is to keep people convinced that part of their money should be invested in something without risk, such as conservative 5% to 6% fixed income investments.

Glenny was your typical savvy millionaire. Glenny drove a 5 year old mid-line Mercedes while his wife drove a 10 year old Lexus. They lived in a $300,000 home with no mortgage. He owned several businesses, but paid himself a modest salary under six figures. He invested the rest. His number one rule was to always save, and he did — millions of dollars. I consider that an excellent habit.

Another good habit of Glenny's was to make sure his portfolio was always invested in a conservative tilt and that his investments were always allocated with an asset allocation strategy. Glenny always kept true to his allocation strategy, even though we were in the midst of the great technology boom then. Many investors lost a high percentage of their portfolios in 2000 thru 2002 during the bust. Because Glenny had a disciplined investment strategy through all types of markets, the market bust had little effect on his overall portfolio.

Bad Habits

We all wish we could be like the Glenny's of the world, but many common bad financial habits get in the way. Included among these is spending too much money. Just because your salary increases does not mean your spending should too. Trying to keep up with the Jones' can be detrimental to your portfolio.

Another bad habit is the "get rich quick" stock tip. You will hear this trick many times in your life and it will probably be from a colleague without a detailed asset allocation strategy. If you want to invest in these stock tips, make sure it is with mad money that you can afford to lose because most of the time, you do lose it.

Financial Planning: Where to Start?

Start with a monthly budget. The United States of America is considered one of the most prosperous nations in the world, but we have the lowest savings rates for the typical family household. By following my advice, that situation can be avoided because you will make more than you will spend. Overspending to keep up with the Jones' is a common mistake made in the professional world. That is why we start the financial planning process with this basic exercise. As simple as it seems, many people's finances break down at the most crucial part of planning – the budget.

I would advise you to purchase some type of software like Quicken or MSN money to make this process easier. Let us start off on a blank piece of paper. Put down your entire monthly fixed or semi-fixed expenses such as rent or mortgage payments, electricity, utilities, standard grocery bills, etc. Then put together all of your miscellaneous expenses. Next, let us look at your income after taxes and insurances (net take home pay).

Doctor Example's Monthly Budget:

Monthly Net Income = $12,000

Mortgage on home	$2000
Extra on principal	$ 200
Student loan	$1000
Car Note	$ 700
Utilities	$ 800
Groceries	$1000
Phone	$ 150
Insurance (car)	$ 300
Miscellaneous ins.	$ 200
Fun Money	<u>$1000</u>

TOTAL $7,350

Savings = $4,650 ($12,000 - $7,350)

Can you see the amount that should be going into savings? The general rule is to have 3 to 6 months worth of expenses in an emergency fund savings account. This physician should have at least $22,050 with a goal of $44,100 in a short term

CD, money market, or savings account that can be accessed very easily without penalty.

Lifestyle Questions

You will be, or are currently, working very hard and would probably like to realize some of the fruits of your labor. How do most people reward themselves for their personal achievements: material objects? They upgrade to the new Mercedes, a bigger house, or the latest electronic gadgets. The majority of your possessions do not make you rich by increasing your net worth. They just make you look like you have worth. What I am trying to accomplish with this book is to help you put your efforts towards increasing your net worth instead of just your belongings. A question that you should ask yourself before making a big purchase is, "Is this an *appreciating asset?*" and "Will this increase my net worth?"

Life Goals

Here is a great exercise that you have been doing for many years and probably did not realize you were doing it. At one point in your life, you decided to become a doctor. This decision led you to design a game plan to get accepted into medical school long before you were even eligible to apply. You did not just stumble into your position like so many people do with their investments or retirement. Now apply this same goal-oriented decision making method to your financial planning efforts.

First, start off by looking at your current situation. Take an inventory of your assets (what you own and the fair market value if you sold it today) and your liabilities (what you owe, loans, mortgages, etc). Now take your assets less your liabilities. That value is your Net Worth.

Assets – Liabilities = Net Worth

Next, project the value of your ideal net worth five years from now. Then, envision your net worth goals ten years from now. Let's think of this differently. What will your net worth need to be in order to live the lifestyle you desire? After you put this to paper, you should then figure out what has to happen in order for you to obtain these goals. A CERTIFIED FINANCIAL PLANNER™ practitioner should be able to step in and help you at this point.

The idea behind financial planning is to start planning and implementing now. Realizing your future values and goals ahead of time will allow you to achieve them with comfort and success.

17

Chapter 2
Loans and Borrowing

Student Loans vs. Credit Card Debt

Generally speaking, when you take out a loan or acquire debt, try to evaluate what type of benefit you will derive from that debt. Let me provide you with an example of deriving benefit out of debt. The benefit of a student loan is an education. An education provides the ability to obtain a high earning job to pay off that loan as well as the ability to maintain worth thereafter. However, not all debts create such lasting benefits.

The problem with credit card debt is that most individuals or families with credit cards spend money they do not have on goods that do not appreciate, such as going out to eat, televisions, or other depreciating consumer goods. This is unlike the student loan where *the student* represents the asset, and as a result of the loan, derives the benefit of having the knowledge and ability to make increasing returns. As for credit cards, many families are drowning in debt for which there is no lasting benefit. Credit card companies are allowed to charge an enormous amount of fees on top of your debt, which in some cases is up to the 22 to 23 percent range. In these cases, the debt, fees, and interest all snowball, making it extremely hard for families to recover.

For these reasons, credit cards should be avoided unless you can pay the balance in full each month. By paying off your debt each month, you are simply using the credit card company's money to purchase goods. Meanwhile, you are accumulating cash in your money market or savings account and you accumulate interest for that month. Then, you can go ahead and pay off that credit card each month and not have to worry about accruing any credit card interest. The reason you will not accrue interest is because most credit card companies will not charge interest to any balance paid in full within the billing periods. They only charge interest to balances that run over. If you never let your balance run over, then you are possibly using your credit card in a valuable, appreciable manner.

If you still want to obtain a credit card, consider one that has rewards or a points system so that you can benefit from it, not pay interest, and achieve a win-win outcome. An example is the American Express Hilton Honors card that, at this particular time, does not have fees.

If you were to stay at a Hilton hotel or an affiliated chain, you would receive a certain amount of points every time you used your Hilton Honors card. You can benefit by using this type of credit card if you pay off each bill at the end of the month, use it for household expenses, and meanwhile accumulate points. You can then use these points towards benefits such as weeks of vacation at a Hilton resort.

Understand that if you are going to use a credit card, do it smartly and don't carry a balance. Another credit card feature to be cautious of is 0% introductory rates. Use this feature if you know you can pay off the balance in the time period allotted. Some credit cards offer a 3.9 percent fixed rate on balances until paid off, which could possibly be an advantage for you if you do have debt charging higher interest rates. However, keep in mind that these rates can be changed at any time at the discretion of the credit card company. Always remember to be cautious.

Buying a Home or Other Major Purchase

Home Purchasing
When it comes to buying a home, consider one that has the potential to appreciate in value

and further increase your net worth. I understand that buying a home that you are comfortable in and happy with is a difficult decision in itself. How do you know if the home you choose will appreciate in value? Thomas Stanley, author of *The Millionaire Mind*, advises to avoid buying the "biggest house" in the neighborhood (unless you plan on living in that house for the rest of your life). If you do get the biggest house in the neighborhood, most likely you will receive a limited amount of appreciation in the property's value compared to the rest of the neighborhood. Stanley suggests that if you find a nice neighborhood and buy the *smallest* house at the lowest price, you will have the property with the most potential to appreciate because the surrounding neighborhood will raise the property value.

When buying a new home, first figure out how much you can actually afford to put down. The standard amount is 20 percent, but you can do much less than that with Federal Housing Authority loans, especially loans for first time home purchasers.

The next step to take is actually shopping the rates. The difference between a bank and a mortgage broker is a mortgage broker can shop the rates from a wide variety of financial institutions.

Now, let us look at the bank as the lender for your mortgage. Sometimes when you go with a lender such as your bank, you need to be careful that they offer the lowest rates because you are not going to have many choices, especially with that type of loan structure.

If you go to a mortgage lender, most of the time they will be able to shop the rates of all the different banks. Nevertheless, you need to inquire about all the fees involved with your mortgage. A financial planner should be able to help you shop these rates and advise you in what direction would be best for your mortgage.

Another consideration before purchasing is putting down 20 percent of the appraised value of the home. By doing this you will avoid Private Mortgage Insurance, PMI.

This insurance is more of a menace than anything else. PMI insurance is an extra monthly insurance that goes on your bill. For example, with a house that cost a couple hundred thousand dollars, you are talking about probably over 100 dollars a month for this insurance. This monthly expense can be avoided by putting down at least 20 percent up front.

Other Major Purchases

When making a major purchase, like buying a boat or vehicle, keep in mind that in most cases these are not appreciating assets. Again, when you are trying to increase your net worth like the true rich do, you want to consider purchases that will help achieve that goal. Assets such as cars usually do not.

Also, beware of any type of timeshare or condo purchase. You need to know when you can use that purchase and how it is going to benefit you. Many people get talked into timeshare purchases that may not be good for their net worth.

A very popular asset you may be tempted to buy is rental property. In certain instances this can prove to be a profitable purchase, but at other times the result is quite the opposite. A number of questions need to be addressed before you invest or purchase this type of asset:

1. *Location:* Is the property in a location that you will be able to monitor and understand the market without much difficulty?
2. *Management:* Are you prepared to collect rent, hire maintenance operators, and prepare lease/rental contracts?
3. *Overall Benefit:* What type of true return or benefit will you receive?

These are crucial questions that need to be answered before this type of purchase. If you are considering using the property as a vacation home you need to be very familiar with the current tax law. Anytime you are considering using an investment for tax purposes, make sure you take into account that your annual income may disqualify you for certain tax breaks. Many itemized deductions are not available for high income earners such as deducting your mortgage interest. If it is considered a vacation home you can rent it out for fewer than 15 days and not have to report any rental income or deduct any rental expenses. You can find additional information on this topic at www.irs.gov. (*Tax Topic 415, Renting Vacation Property/Renting to Relatives and Publication 527* , *Residential Rental Property (including Rental of Vacation Homes).*

Should I Have Debt?

A big question for many families is "Should I even have debt?" Some experts advise not to have any debt-to-cash ratio, have everything paid off. Then others say, "There is good debt and there is bad debt." I agree with the latter comment in that depending on your individual level of comfort, there are both good and bad types of debt.

Let us reflect on our previous example of good debt: student loans. Student loans are appreciated assets that will help you in future years. In addition, if you obtain loans at 2 to 3 percent on your liquid cash and earn higher interest on other investments, then you are actually ahead of the game.

So to end this section, if you have debt remember these three main points:

1. Make sure that the debt is on an appreciable asset.
2. The debt is controllable.
3. The debt is at a low interest rate.

Saving for the Kids

It has been said that it is never too early to start saving for your child's education expenses. As costs of education escalate, it is important to know the tools available to save for future education expenses.

529 Plan

A great savings tool for higher education is the 529 plan. There are mutual fund companies contracted with certain states to offer such plans. The benefits of a 529 plan are that you can contribute a maximum of $55,000 per year, which will grow tax-deferred and can be taken out tax-free as long as the money is used for college expenses. Another great feature with the 529 plan is the control feature. With this, you control the asset and have the ability to shift savings from one child to another as needed.

NOTE: An investor should consider the investment objectives, risks, and charges and expenses associated with municipal fund securities before investing. More information about municipal fund securities is available in the issuer's official statement and the official statement should be read carefully before investing.

ESA Coverdell

Other types of plans include the Coverdell ESA (Educational Savings Account) for kids;

however, most physicians probably make too much money to be able to utilize this tool. The modified adjusted annual gross income phase out for married people filing jointly is between $190,000 and $220,000. Also, the maximum contribution is only $2,000 per student. An added benefit for this type of account is that the saved funds can be used for any type of educational expenses, including grammar school. The invested funds grow tax-deferred and can be taken out tax-free as long as the money is used for educational expenses.

Custodial Accounts

Some people are interested in having a custodial account set up on behalf of their children. A UGMA (Uniformed Gifts to Minors Act) or UTMA (Uniform Transfers to Minors Act) would probably be used for these purposes. These types of accounts currently do not give any tax benefits, but they are the only way a child can hold assets. The custodian, usually one of the parents, makes all of the financial and investment decisions regarding the account. UGMA accounts need to be moved to the child's name and possession at 18 years of age. These changes take place at 21 years of age for the UTMA. These rules should be taken into account when considering this type of plan.

Chapter 3
Insurance: How Much and For What?

I am a firm believer in the mantra "hope for the best, but prepare for the worst." This is especially true if you are going to be a high income earner, which usually means owner of valuable assets and payer of increased expenses. You need to make sure that you, your assets, your family, and your businesses are monetarily protected. This protection can be provided by obtaining liability insurance.

Liability Insurance

There are several forms of liability insurance that need to be considered including homeowners' insurance and umbrella policies.

First, let us consider your homeowners' insurance coverage. When looking at homeowners' policies, you should take into account a policy that is going to be able to cover your home's replacement costs and all of your valuables. Then, on top of that type of insurance, you should look at an umbrella policy.

An umbrella policy provides coverage for costs that exceed the limits on your homeowners' policies and also on your car insurance policies. In order for the umbrella policy to be beneficial, make sure you are insured at the highest limits with your car insurance. The highest limit is 250,000 - 500,000 - 250,000.

For example, if, heaven-forbid, you are at fault in a multi-car collision and everyone in the collision drives a high-cost vehicle and injuries are sustained and you get sued — would your insurance provide adequate coverage? If the amount of damage exceeds the amount of your policies, then the plaintiff's attorney will come after your personal assets. That is when the umbrella policy comes into play. You can purchase the umbrella policy in increments of $1 million, $2 million, etc. The cost of these policies are minimal, and in some cases, only a couple hundred to a few hundred dollars a year. Again, this is just-in-case protection. I believe it is very important to protect your assets and the umbrella policy is one way to be covered.

The Value of Life: Discovering Your Life Insurance Needs

Life is your most important asset. For all practicing physicians alike, income is based upon the services provided to patients. In the unfortunate event that something happens to you, it is necessary to know how this income loss will affect your family. How do you put a price on your most valued asset?

Determining an estimated amount of necessary life insurance can actually be quite simple. The first step is taking inventory of your current assets (liquid assets that can be sold) and your current liabilities. Here's an example:

Dr. Provider

Asset		*Liability*	
House	$350k	Mortgage	$250k
Car	$25k	Car Loan	$20k
Investment Acct	$50k	Student Loan	$120k
Savings	$35k	Personal Loans	$10k
TOTAL	*$460k*	*TOTAL*	*$400k*

(Assets - liabilities = Net Worth) **Net Worth = $60k**

Most likely, Dr. Provider's spouse will not sell the house and car, greatly decreasing the significance of its fair market value in the life insurance equation. Let us look at the current liabilities in the example: $400k. If you subtract from this amount the investment account and savings assets, you are left with approximately $315,000 of debt upon your death. Then, include an additional $30,000 for burial expenses which gives a new total of $345k. So, Dr. Provider needs at least $345,000 just for his family to break even.

The next step in estimating an adequate amount of life insurance is to calculate the income amount necessary to keep the family at a certain standard of living. Dr. Provider needs a minimum total of $6k per month to maintain their current lifestyle. That adds up to $72k per year (not including inflation).

The simple equation for calculating the entire amount of life insurance is to divide the yearly amount of $72k by 4.5% (reasonable rate of return) equaling $1,600,000. Add in the $345,000 of debt to the $1,600,000 to reach a grand total of $1,945,000.

Dr. Provider should obtain a life insurance policy that will insure his life for at least $2 million. Applying this method leads to a simplified way you can estimate the amount of life insurance necessary without adding inflation to the mix.

Term Insurance Policy

Many different types of life insurance policies exist. One type of policy, which is the least expensive, is a term insurance policy. A term insurance policy is usually for a certain amount of years of coverage during which you can lock in the amount of premium payments. When you choose a term policy, the life insurance gives you a guarantee of the actual death proceeds to be paid to your beneficiaries if you die within the coverage period. Thus, with a term policy you pay your premiums for the years stated on the policy, and if you pass away during that time period, your beneficiaries will get the full death benefit of the policy.

Permanent Insurance Policy

Another type of insurance is a permanent policy. Permanent policies are whole life, variable life, or universal life policies. With permanent policies, you are essentially buying insurance and then receiving some type of investment or interest rate that you are going to get inside the policy. The policy is considered a permanent policy because there are no term limits on the policy. It does not expire unless there is nothing left of value in the policy. These types of policies have what is known as cash values and corresponding investment perks. Many of these policies allow you to borrow against the cash values or finance additional insurance through the cash value.

The downside to permanent policies is that it may take several years for you to start seeing any real cash value in the policy because of the expenses. However, after many years with the permanent policy, you may be able to use the cash value to pay for future premiums, borrow against the cash value tax-free, or simply withdraw cash value in future years.

When looking into these policies ask yourself, "Should I use a term policy and invest the savings in another type of investment with fewer expenses, or should I just invest in a permanent policy?" One large advantage with a permanent policy compared to the term is the cash value of a permanent policy is protected from creditors. But then again, the same is true for retirement accounts and annuities.

Disability Income Insurance

Most people do not understand the necessity of disability income insurance. Most individuals understand the importance of life, home, auto, and health insurance, but do not perceive disability insurance on the same level of importance. For those who think disability insurance is less important than health or life, please read the following statistics about disability:

- One in three employees will become disabled for 90 days or more before age 65.
- One in seven employees will be disabled for five years or more before retirement.
- At age 32, a disability of three months or longer

before age 65 is six times more likely than death.
("Commissioner's Individual Disability Table A").

After studying the above statistics, you can see that disability insurance policies provide a very important type of insurance coverage for your family.

There are different types of disability insurance policies and there are different types of disability features you can have on a policy. One feature is "own occupation." This feature is essential because if you were to become disabled the insurance company would pay your losses. Before we get too far ahead, let us define "disabled" under an own occupation policy. Being disabled means not being able to perform your current job. Any other definition will allow the insurance company to expect you to do another job.

Let me give you an example: A physician develops an allergy to latex. Well, under this condition the physician is disabled from performing his normal job due to his inability to use latex gloves. So, with the own occupation feature, he would qualify as disabled. However, if he had the "any occupation" definition selected in his policy, the insurance company would not consider him disabled and would expect him to look for a job in research or other work of that nature.

If you are concerned with paying expensive premiums, you have several options, such as the non-cancelable, "noncan," feature. This guarantees the physician can keep the policy in force by paying a premium which will not increase. Another beneficial feature would be "guaranteed renewable." This means the premiums may be increased on a class basis. The premiums of the guaranteed renewable feature will be less when compared to the noncan feature. Some additional features are the elimination or waiting period. Keep in mind the longer the waiting period, the less expensive the premium. Waiting period refers to the time that lapses from the time you are considered disabled to the time the insurance company payouts your checks. So, if you generally have a decent amount of cash or liquid investments that could sustain your standard of living for a while, make the waiting period as long as possible to lower your premiums.

The last feature is the cost-of-living adjustments (COLAs). COLA's usually cost an additional premium, but I believe it is well worth it. This is the increase in benefits on a certain percentage basis of the monthly checks because of the cost of living. You want this feature because the cost of living is steadily increasing, so we want the disability checks to also increase.

Long-Term Care Insurance

Long-term care insurance has become increasingly popular over the past several years.

One of the main reasons is because we are living longer and the baby boomers are starting to see their elderly parents needing long term care facilities or home care. If your assets are substantial, you may be able to self insure: meaning use your own assets to cover the future cost of long term care.

The following is an article I wrote regarding this topic:

"The Long-Term Care Impact on Your Retirement"

Many people understand the significance of having catastrophic health care coverage or life insurance, but do not understand how the lack of long-term care coverage could devastate a family and their savings. Long-term care can be paid for in three different ways: Personal savings, the government (Medicaid), or Long-Term Care Insurance.

Personal Savings
The U.S. Department of Health and Human Services estimates that about 40% of people aged 65 or older have at least a 50% lifetime risk of entering a nursing home. Currently, the average cost of a private room in a nursing home is $192 per day or about $70,000 annually. Let us see how this affects a retirement portfolio. Example: Dr. Smith has a retirement

portfolio of $1 million. He takes $50,000 of income off of the portfolio which returns 5%. With this scenario, he never runs out of money (if all things are equal) by living on the interest or return of the portfolio. However, if Dr. Smith needs long-term care at a cost of $70,000 per year combined with his $50,000 of retirement income, then his total portfolio will be depleted in 11 years.

The Government

The government pays for long-term care costs through Medicare and Medicare supplemental coverage, also known as Medigap insurance. Standard health insurance policies do not cover long-term care. Medicaid will cover long-term care only if all assets have been depleted while having little or no income. Doing this is highly not recommended.

Long-Term Care Insurance

Long-term care insurance can be viewed as a solid investment for those who have assets to protect or who want to avoid becoming a financial burden to their families. Long-term care insurance includes a range of nursing, social, and rehabilitative services for people who need ongoing assistance due to a chronic illness or disability. Long-term care insurance can be used by anyone at any age who suffers an accident or debilitating illness. However, it is most frequently used by older adults who need assistance with essential physical needs, such as bathing, dressing, or eating.

Most long-term care policies are "expense-incurred," meaning they pay a fixed-dollar amount toward the cost of daily care. Policies tend to cover a variety of care settings, including nursing homes, home health care, assisted living facilities and adult day care. Premium costs increase depending on your age at the time of enrollment. This means that the younger you are when you purchase a policy, the lower the premium you are likely to pay.

In conclusion, with modern medicine we are living longer and need to plan for longer lives which in many cases will be with some type of help whether it is a nursing home or home nursing. Nevertheless, when it comes to financial planning, you always plan for the worse and hope for the best.

Chapter 4
Investment Planning

What Are The Different Classes Of Assets?

When it comes to investing their money, many people are content with taking a random approach. They may have received a hot tip on a particular investment and decided to plow a large amount of money into it with no regard for the overall balance of their portfolios. However, research has shown that it is through the careful selection of various asset classes rather than the individual investments themselves that people prosper financially. One study found that on average as much as 91.5 percent of an investment portfolio's overall return can be attributed to asset class selection.[1] Therefore, the careful selection and

Chad Olivier, CFP®

distribution of your investments among the various asset classes is crucial to the future success of your investment portfolio.

There are five broad asset classes that you should take into consideration when constructing your investment portfolio.

1. *Cash*

The term "cash" refers to the most liquid holdings in your portfolio. It includes checking account balances, money market funds, and certificates of deposit. Conventional wisdom holds that you should keep three to six months worth of salary in cash to cover yourself in the event of an emergency.

2. *Fixed-Principal Investments*

This class consists of investments that do not put your principal at risk to market forces. Fixed annuities and trust deeds fall into this category.

3. *Debt*

Debt includes municipal, corporate, and government agency bonds. The class also covers other debt-secured investments such as collateralized mortgage obligations.

4. *Equity*

The fourth class termed "equity" represents an ownership interest in a business entity. This class covers any investment you might make in stocks or a stock-oriented mutual fund. It also covers any interest you may have in a closely held corporation or partnership.

42

5. *Tangibles*

The fifth class, tangibles, includes your holdings in real estate, art, gold, precious stones, stamps, baseball cards, or other valuable collector's items.

How you choose to distribute your investments among the various asset classes depends on your goals, your risk tolerance, and your expected rate of return. Keep in mind that asset allocation does not guarantee against loss; it is a method used to manage risk.

1 Source: Brinson, Singer, and Beebower, "Determinants of Portfolio Performance II: An I Update," Financial Analysts Journal, May-June 1991.

Investment Pyramid

Portfolio Pyramid Model

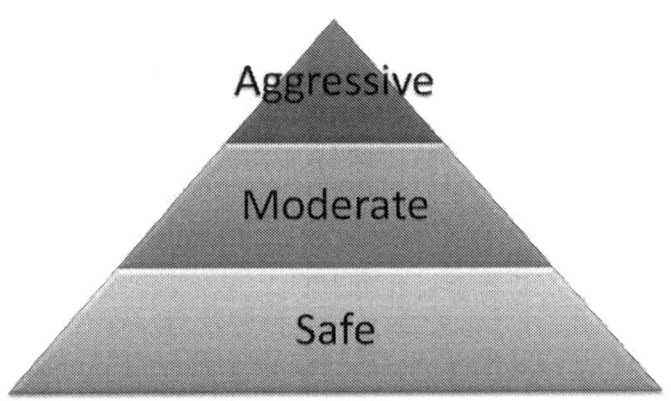

The Portfolio Pyramid Model shows the proper portfolio allocation for your overall investments. Your investments should be balanced in a pyramid formation, with the riskier items on top and the conservative investments building the foundation. As you climb the investment pyramid, the returns will tend to have more potential to increase. Notice I said potential because they could just as well decrease.

Think of investing like maintaining a good diet. You can not eat a high percentage of sweets and expect to maintain a healthy body. Investing works much to the same effect: You can not invest in a high percentage of risky assets and expect to maintain a successful portfolio. So give yourself a hearty portion of safe investments, with a decent side of moderate investments, and a small dessert of risk.

The Base of Your Investments

The bottom portion of the pyramid consists of a montage of different conservative investments. The investments in this portion should be the bulk of your investment assets. This will consist of short-term fixed income investments (savings, certificate of deposits, bonds) that will be stable with consistent growth.

Intermediate (Middle Investments)

The middle section of your portfolio pyramid is where the real estate or big blue chip mutual funds come into play. This category could be very large. There are many different types of investments and mutual funds or money managers that could possibly fit in this category.

Be cautious of the duplications of investments and investment styles. Many investors believe they are quite diversified because they have many different mutual funds. Nevertheless, many times these funds hold the same securities and make your portfolio concentrated and as a result, potentially devastating the portfolio in certain market downturns.

High Risk

The top of your portfolio pyramid consists of investments with higher risk tolerance. This includes small to mid capitalization companies, perhaps a portion of managed futures funds, and what is called 'get rich quick' stock picks.

The high risk piece will be by far the smallest segment of your total asset picture and maintaining that portion size is crucial. This is where the money that you can afford to lose is invested. If you do lose it, it will not be detrimental to you, and if it does well, then that will be beneficial for your portfolio. Many problems can arise if a high percentage of investment dollars sit at the top of the pyramid. This is a common problem. There are many imprudent advisors whose portfolios have too many bad investments. Often times, basic investment philosophies are broken in these situations, including sell your losers and keep your winners. Most people do the opposite.

Investment Vehicles

Today's investor has several investment vehicles to examine when comparing the portfolio. Let us start at the bottom of the Portfolio Pyramid again with fixed income investments.

Fixed Income

Fixed income investments include bonds, CDs, and money markets. This is where interest is accruing. For example, when purchasing a bond or CD, you are actually loaning money to a corporation or bank that is going to give you a certain amount of income and then generally give you your money back after a specified period of time or the borrowing entity gives the par amount back. Par amount for bonds is 1,000 dollars per bond.

Depending on what type of interest rate environment you are in, you may sometimes pay a little bit more to buy the bond. If you bought a bond for $1,010, which is for a premium, you will then get $1,000 dollars back when the bond matures. The reason why you will be paying a premium for the bond is because interest rates have gone down. So, you will be paying a premium to receive the higher coupon payments associated with that particular bond.

Do Not Be Afraid to Invest in CDs

I would like to expand on a side note regarding CDs while we are discussing asset classes. You may be thinking, "Why would anyone be afraid of CDs?" Well, the concern lies not in the safety of principal and return, but in the perception given by Wall Street and the media that the majority of someone's money needs to be in stocks to gain real returns.

Just recently, I was watching one of the financial networks on which an investor forum was starting, with the audience asking questions to a panel of investment professionals from large brokerage firms' advisory services. Whenever someone from the audience asked questions about asset allocation types, one representative's response was always focused on needing a large percentage in equities (stocks). This completely baffled me. It is a given that in these types of situations the person answering forum questions needs to remain vague. Nevertheless, what I got out of this forum is that we should all have a majority of equities in our portfolio.

Now, let me explain to you why the fixed income market may be a good choice to include in your investment portfolio. In general, physicians make a very good living with consistent growth. A Certificate of Deposit (CD) is in the first asset class cash. A CD is FDIC insured up to $100k and will give a yield plus your money back at a certain time in the future.

Now, in 2006 we saw what is known as an inverted yield curve which means the short-term yields were higher than the long-term yields. So, in this economic environment, we are seeing the short-term CDs yielding over 5%, while the longer maturity CDs are yielding much less. If your goal is to average a 7% return over time, why not grab some FDIC guaranteed yields of 5% for a percentage of the overall portfolio, then work your way up the pyramid to try and capture the rest of the return.

When an inverted yield curve exists in the markets, an investor can take advantage of the shifting of the curve. When the long term yields begin to increase above the short term yields, it signifies a good time to purchase long term bonds 10 to 15 years out. One way to purchase long term bonds is to let a money manager (or mutual fund manager) purchase these bonds by investing with a fund manager that has these objectives or, alternatively, you could buy the bonds and add them to your portfolio individually.

The advantage of owning the individual bonds is that it is a debt obligation directly to you. This means that when you buy the bond, you lock in on the interest rate and the promise to receive $1000 per bond at maturity. With the mutual fund portfolio alternative, this promise and advantage is forgone. The mutual fund portfolio is generally intended for the manager to trade the bonds using his expertise while you benefit by receiving an overall total return from the portfolio.

A positive aspect of the shifting of the yield curve is that as interest rates begin to drop, the value of the bonds will increase. In a falling interest rate environment, the longer term bonds will see a very good percentage of appreciation in the price.

Benefits of Investing in REITs

The next type of investment to look at would be the real estate investment trust. Real estate investment trusts are trusts of different real estate holdings depending on the objectives of the particular trust. The majority of them pay income and then you would have some type of appreciation with that depending on the goals of that trust.

People have utilized real estate as an investment throughout history. When considering buying real estate, most investors are hesitant because of the monitoring and time involved in such a purchase. Nevertheless, diversifying in the real estate market can help stabilize returns in your investment portfolio. There is a way to invest in real estate and not have to worry about collecting rent or getting dreadful phone calls to unclog your tenant's toilet. This balance can be reached through investing in Real Estate Investment Trusts, also known as REITs. Many varieties of REITs exist, including privately held offerings (not actively traded) and public offerings on the open market (trade on a stock exchange). Instead of purchasing a single piece of property, the REIT enables the investor to pool his or her money with other investors and purchase many properties, with professional management companies collecting rents and handling problems. The following are additional benefits:

- Reliable Monthly Income: Because REITs are required to pay out most taxable income as dividends, these companies generally offer higher dividend payouts and yields than most other public companies.

- Tax Advantaged Opportunities: When you invest in commercial properties, a "pass through" of property depreciation allows a certain percentage of the income to be treated as tax deferred.

- Diversification from Stock Market Volatility: A study released last year by Ibbotson Associates demonstrates that because of their low correlation to other types of investments, REITs can help lower portfolio risk and potentially increase portfolio returns.

- Potential Capital Preservation and Appreciation: REITs typically have higher dividend yield than most equity investments. There are several factors responsible for this yield. As much as two-thirds of REIT total return comes in the form of cash dividends. Of the various REIT properties available, neighborhood and community shopping centers are believed by many to be among the most recession-resistant. This is due in part to their long lease terms which are typically 15 to 20 years. The length of the lease term works to provide a relatively secure income stream. Also, the type of tenants that retail centers attract enhances the safety and stability of the property portfolio. Further, many neighborhood and community shopping centers are anchored by large grocery stores and/or discount stores. These "anchor" stores are tenants that generally perform well during economic downturns.

Due to the number of benefits to investing in REITs, adding REITs to an investment portfolio may provide increased diversification. After all, the key to investment performance is diversification. The REIT provides a unique balance to the investor who desires real estate property return without the headache of having to deal with the day to day tenant issues.

NOTE: Investing in REITs/real estate involves special risks such as illiquidity. REITs should only be used as part of a diversified portfolio, as they may not be suitable for everyone. There is no assurance the investment objectives of the program will be attained. The principal value of the shares may fluctuate such that at redemption, shares may be worth more or less than the original investment.

Equity Positions (Stocks)

Now let's look at equity type position. Notice I am saying equity type position. This can get confusing, so let me try and make it easy to understand. The basic definition of a stock (equity) is that you are part owner in a company. You are considered a shareholder of that company. Some equities give off dividends and some do not. The idea of equities is that you are buying it and hoping that it does appreciate at a later value. At that time, you would sell it and get your gain from the appreciation.

One way to invest with equities while having a more diversified portfolio is through mutual funds. Mutual funds give you the ability to buy shares in the fund, then the fund manager buys multiple shares in the equities and buys and sells them as he sees fit. Generally, funds come with some type of fee for the service. With the mutual funds, you could have funds that have debt obligations like bonds or a mixture of both bonds and equities.

When you own the actual CD or the bond, you get par value back at a certain date. The downfall of having the portfolio inside the mutual fund is that you do not actually own the CD or bonds. The mutual company does. As a result, you do not have the security of actually getting your money back at a specified date. They are investing on the dividends and the appreciation by constantly selling and buying the bond portfolio inside the mutual fund. This could be a downfall with investing in bond type mutual funds.

One thing to look at when you are considering investing is what the money will be used for. If you are looking at retirement, you have many, many years away. That does not mean you should become aggressive because you still have many years away. You need to look at a diversified portfolio with asset allocation. On the other hand, if you are expecting a short-term need for money, then you must look at putting money in some type of short-term fixed income investment or something that you know the money would be available if you actually need it.

The Portfolio

Begin with the basics when developing or modifying a portfolio. The Portfolio Pyramid, as discussed above, outlines basic principles when diversifying assets. Work your way up the pyramid with specific investments. Always stay true to the pyramid. Let us look at an example:

Dr. A is a 45 year old physician.
His annual salary is $500k.

He is married with 3 children.
He has a retirement account valued at $600k.
Investment nonretirement accounts are $800k.
Monthly expenses of $10k.
Risk tolerate is moderate.

First, we know Dr. A should have 6 months of expenses liquid for emergencies, as we discussed earlier. This would equal at least $60k in short term CDs, savings, or money markets. His risk tolerance is moderate which means he should be more conservative. A possible portfolio for Dr. A is shown below:

5% ($70k)	Microcap stocks, Tech
10% ($140k)	Managed Futures, Small Cap funds, Mid Cap, Spec bonds
30% ($420k)	REITs, Equity funds (large cap), Corporate bonds, Bond funds, Total Return fund
55% ($770k)	Savings, Money market, AAA bonds, Government bonds

As you can see, this Portfolio Pyramid can have many investment choice possibilities. Some investments merge into others within the pyramid. The top, aggressive portion of the pyramid could have a mutual fund that incorporates small and mid caps, but will also have a certain percentage in micro and technology stocks. Thus, choosing investments in each of the pyramid's categories does not have to be so cut and dry. You have options, but it is important to work within the determined percentages in order to achieve a consistent return.

When investing, consider what the money will be used for. If you are looking at retirement, even though you may be many years away does not mean you should become aggressive. You need to look at a diversified portfolio with asset allocation. On the other hand, if you are expecting a short term need for money, then you must look at putting money in some type of short term fixed income investment or something that you know the money would be available if you if necessary.

Investment Policy Statement

An Investment Policy Statement (IPS) should be used when constructing a portfolio. The investment policy statement explains how a portfolio will be managed. The IPS is usually derived from a financial plan, which provides information about what return a given portfolio will need to average in order to achieve the investor's stated goals. Using information about that return, an Investment Policy Statement should be developed. The IPS will have specific ranges of equity, fixed income, and alternative investments that should be followed to achieve a stated return. The following is an example of the portfolio portion of an IPS:

ACCEPTABLE RANGE OF COMMITMENT

	Max	Min	Target
Total Equities	60%	20%	40%
Total Fixed Income	75%	20%	40%
Alternative Investments	30%	10%	20%

This portfolio provides a target range of 40% in equities. Thus, if there should be a market run and your equity portfolio starts to do very well, the IPS would not allow the portfolio to become over-weighted in equity holdings. In this situation, some equities will be sold and moved to the other two categories of assets in order to bring the portfolio back within target range. What this does for the portfolio is shorten the ranges of returns, and as a result, help achieve the stated goal return. Keep in mind the portfolio should stay within those ranges, and if it goes outside of the ranges, it must be readjusted.

By having an Investment Policy Statement in place, you and your financial planner will be working with specific goals and procedures to manage your investment account. This will protect your investment portfolio from losing balance, and in turn, protect your wealth.

Chapter 5
Retirement Planning

Retirement planning has evolved over the years. The choices you make today help lead you down the right path toward a comfortable retirement tomorrow. Retirement plans can be broken down into two basic categories: the defined contribution plan and the defined benefit plan.

Defined Contribution Plan

As stated in the name, this plan is based on the contributions made by either the employer or employee. There are different subcategories of defined contribution plans. Let us start with the simplest and work our way to the more complicated plan types.

Simple IRA

The simple IRA is for small employers, including employers with 100 or less employees. It requires employers to match employee contributions. With simple IRAs, the amount the employer matches is immediately invested, meaning that if the employee leaves the company, the employee gets to keep the employer amount that was contributed. The contribution limit for this plan is $10,000 and the company can not utilize any other plan, which can be a very big disadvantage. On the contrary, the Simple IRA does not allow the investor to combine profit sharing plans as well as defined benefit plans.

SEP IRA

This plan can be ideal for small, one to two person offices. With SEP IRAs, the employer is the only one making contributions, which is up to 25% for owner (W-2) or up to 20% contribution for self-employed. The percentage amount that needs to be contributed for all employees should match what the owner contributes for him or herself. These contributions will be immediately vested, meaning that an employee can possibly leave the employer with a big contribution from the employer. This could be a very costly liability for a business.

401(k) Plan

This is one of the more popular retirement plans. The 401k plan is ideal for medium to large practices. This plan allows you to put $15,000 employee contributions with a $5,000 catch up for individuals over 50 years of age. 401k plans can be established with a vesting schedule for the employer contributions, which end up being anywhere from 3 to 6% of the employees' salary. With the 401k plan, there are ways to add additional plans such as a profit-sharing plan. This will enable the high income earners to maximize a plan that will put the total contributions to $15k (employee contribution) plus possibly another $29k (employer contribution). When using 401k plans, you want to avoid having a plan that is discriminatory. You can do this by making the plan a Safe Harbor plan.

Money-Purchase Plan

The Money-Purchase Plan (MPP) was very popular years ago, but has been replaced by the 401k/profit-sharing plan. The money-purchase plan is ideal for businesses with consistent cash flow. The employer can contribute up to 25%, but the contributions are *fixed* once the percentage rate is set. Therefore, it is important that cash flows are consistent because the MPP plan does not offer any flexibility or "wiggle" room. The maximum contribution will be 100% of salary or $44,000 plus $5,000 catch up for individuals over 50 years of age. This plan is ideal for highly compensated, relatively young employees.

Target Benefit Plan (TBP)

The target benefit plan allows up to 25%

employer deduction with fixed contributions. Again, similar to the money-purchase plan, the business must have stable cash flows. The TBP favors older employees. The TBP plan looks like a defined benefit plan, but is still limited to the maximum allowable defined contribution plan limits. The maximum contribution will be 100% of salary or $44,000 plus $5,000 catch up for individuals over 50 years of age. The retirement benefit is determined by the account balance and the employee assumes all of the investment risk. If an employee leaves the business, his or her forfeitures may be reallocated to reduce employer contributions.

Profit-Sharing Plan

A profit-sharing plan is used in conjunction with many 401k plans in order to maximize contributions to the highly compensated physicians in the plan. This plan is attractive because it is purely discretionary. The discretionary feature allows an employer to cancel contributions for the year if the practice can not afford to share in the profits. However, if an excessive amount of years go by without a contribution, the IRS may claim the plan has been terminated.

Roth 401(k)

In 2006, the Roth 401(k) came into existence. The Roth 401(k) offers you the ability to put money away that has been taxed and have it grow tax deferred. The catch with a Roth 401(k) is that your money has to be kept away until the age of 59 and ½. The advantage of the Roth 401(k) is that when you take your money out, it will be tax-free (under the condition that it has been in the plan for at least 5 years). Another advantage to this plan is there are no income limits. On the contrary, the Roth IRA penalizes you by not allowing you to invest if you make annually over $160,000 Joint/Married. Below is a section from one of my articles on the subject:

"The Roth 401(k) – Can it Benefit You?"

The Roth IRA, which has been around for many years, excludes families with joint incomes above $150k (it is phased out between $150k and $160k). Whereas, the new Roth 401(k) does not have income limits and can be funded each year with the following maximum funding limits: $15k plus an extra $5k if over the age of 50. So, the lingering question is – should you add this feature to your current 401(k) plan? Let us take a look at an example:

Doctor #1
Age: 40 **Tax bracket:** 35% (Federal) 6% (State)

Roth 401k Contribution	**401k** Contribution
$15 k	$15k
Taxes Paid on Contributions	Taxes Paid on Contributions
$5,250 federal	$0
$900 state	

Assume Doctor #1 retires at age 65, and the investments earn an average of 8%. The total future value would be $406,591, in which the withdrawals will be taxed at the doctor's current tax bracket in retirement for the regular 401(k) contributions, but will be tax free for the Roth 401(k). The big question is whether taxes will be higher in the future – keep in mind the current tax brackets are at one of the lowest levels in history. But, for illustration purposes, let us keep the tax brackets the same as they are currently set.

Withdrawal at Age 65

Roth 401(k) Withdrawal	**401(k)** Withdrawal
$406,591	$406,591
$0 taxes	$142,306.85(federal taxes)
	$24,395.46(state taxes)

The overwhelming benefit for the 40-year-old is the many years of possible compounding growth that can be withdrawn in retirement tax free.

What if you are not 40 years old, and you plan on retiring in the next five to ten years? Will it be beneficial to start the Roth 401(k)? The major benefit for a physician nearing the retirement stage of his/her career is the estate planning benefit. With your current 401(k) and IRAs, after the age of 70 ½ you are forced to withdraw certain percentages of your retirement with the required minimum distribution calculation, which is calculated with current life expectancy tables. With the Roth 401(k) and Roth IRA, there is no required minimum distribution. Therefore, taking advantage of the Roth 401(k) or the Roth IRA could be a way to leave this asset in your estate to pass on tax-free to your heirs. Now keep in mind, if you have a large estate, the Roth asset will be added into the calculation for estate taxes. As a result, more advanced planning should be considered.

If you currently have a 401(k) profit sharing plan, you may want to find out about adding this feature and treading a new path on the road to retirement.

Defined Benefit Plan

One of the main differences between the defined benefit plan and the defined contribution plan is that the benefit plan utilizes the skills of actuaries to predict an income benefit in retirement for the participants in the retirement plan. The benefit plan will pay employees a percentage of their salary for their entire life. The benefit plan can also be combined with the defined contribution plan. If you are in an office with older, highly compensated employees who want to maximize their retirement benefit, this plan can help you. If there is one older doctor and a group of younger employees, this would be very beneficial to the older doctor to add to an existing retirement plan.

The defined benefit plan is becoming extinct because there is a general lack of knowledge and expertise with regard to this type of plan. Many large corporations have both types of plans, but you do not see many small to mid-sized businesses utilizing the defined benefit plan.

Chapter 6
Getting Your Estate in Order

A major consideration for investors with large estates is finding the most beneficial way to transfer their estate to their heirs. Advanced estate planning techniques can help ensure a smooth transfer. One thing you must remember is the government does not need to play fair. What you do and plan for now may not work in the future. Big accounting firms have been scrutinized by the IRS many times for trying to help its clients avoid taxes. This is an area that is very complicated and deserves the utmost attention. If you will owe taxes, you must pay your taxes. So, the technique for efficient planning is not to walk the line or push the envelope, but to stay well within the scope of IRS guidelines.

Estate planning is the most important step to take in the financial planning process. Unfortunately, some investors do not consider estate planning during their financial planning process. Proper estate planning makes the transfer of your estate much easier and ensures that your estate passes on to whom it needs to in the most tax efficient manner.

How would you handle the tax situation of the estate? What are the funeral arrangements? If there are minor children, who is going to be the guardian of the minor children?

Wills

The will automatically dictates how assets will be handled upon death. However, a beneficiary designation on any type of retirement account such as 401k plans, life insurance, or annuities supersedes the formal will.

An example: Dr. Smith has a million dollar life insurance policy that lists his first wife as the beneficiary (assume he purchased the life insurance when they were married and are now divorced). Dr. Smith has a retirement account that lists three children as the primary beneficiary. He creates a will that states he would like all assets to bypass his current wife and go directly to his children. His wife is in agreement with his wishes. Unfortunately, when Dr. Smith passes away, the life insurance proceeds go directly to the first wife, thereby superseding the will.

This is obviously not what Dr. Smith had intended. To avoid this dilemma, ensure that all of your assets (especially the ones that supersede the will such as retirement accounts, IRAs, and life insurance proceeds) list the proper beneficiaries.

Some wills are drafted to include testamentary trusts. In general, testamentary trusts allow the testator, which is the person for whom the will is drafted, to dictate how assets will be controlled, even from the grave. Basically, the assets are held "in trust" by a trustee for the benefit of the beneficiaries for how ever long the trust provides. If you want your 401k or IRA to be included in the assets held in trust, the 401k and IRA need to list the testament trust as the beneficiary.

There are different types of trusts that can be set up. First of all, if you are married, have no children, and you pass away, a simple will sends all of your assets directly to your spouse without bearing any tax consequences. The problem with a simple will is that the first spouse to die does not use up his or her applicable tax exemption amount, which is at $2 million dollars of assets right now.

Everyone should have a last will and testament, especially if you have estate planning needs.

Unified Credit

Unified credit is a credit that taxpayers may use to offset estate and gift taxes. For 2007 and 2008, the Unified Credit Exemption Equivalents for estate tax purposes was $2 million. Keep in mind that the estate tax calculations *include* all assets, like life insurance proceeds, owned by the deceased or the deceased's estate.

Let us take a look at an example:

Dr. Smith's assets at death

Cars..............................$50,000
House...........................$1,000,000
Condo..........................$750,000
Rental Property...............$500,000
Investment Account..........$1,000,000
IRA..............................$3,000,000
Art Collection................$500,000
Furnishings...................$100,000
Bank Accounts................$100,000
Life Insurance Policy........$2,000,000
(Owner: Dr. Smith, Beneficiary: kids)

Estate for planning tax purposes = $9,000,000

Approximate estate tax heirs will owe:
$9 million - $2 million (exemption allowed) = $7 million * 45% = $3,150,000 owed in estate taxes (by the way this is due 9 months after death).

The next question is where his kids will get the money. They will need to liquidate the $1 million investment account plus the $2 million in life insurance proceeds and $100k in the bank. That still leaves $50k to the IRS. The kids should probably try and put in their own money to make up the $50k because if they try to get it from the IRA, then income tax will come into the picture. There are a number of different ways to get the IRA money out the most tax-efficient way possible. The kids may not have a choice.

Where did Dr. Smith go wrong?

1.) *Bad Titling:* He should not own his own life insurance policy. An irrevocable life insurance policy trust should have been created, which would have taken $2 million out of his estate. Just that alone would have saved $900k in estate taxes.

2.) *Advanced planning should have been considered:* Dr. Smith could have possibly done some advanced planning, such as gifting part of the estate to a charity and having the charity purchase a life insurance policy on Dr. Smith with a life insurance trust as the beneficiary for the kids. This would have left a portion of his estate to the charity while providing the kids with tax-free money (lowering the estate burden).

3.) *Planning better in general:* A large portion of

the estate is in nonliquid items. This would make it difficult for the kids to easily come up with estate tax money causing them to use up most of the cash.

Irrevocable Life Insurance Trust

For life insurance policies, an irrevocable life insurance trust should be set up. An irrevocable life insurance trust may be the ideal way to distribute tax-free life insurance proceeds. Remember tax-free life insurance proceeds are included for estate taxes. Yes, you heard me correctly, the proceeds from life insurance policies that you may have will have estate taxes on it if you are not careful. The current estate tax is 45%.

So, what is an Irrevocable Life Insurance Trust? This is where your life insurance policy is held as a trust. Ideally, your beneficiary would receive cash payments from you to purchase your policy now making your beneficiary the trustee. In doing this, you avoid the possibility of your life insurance policy being included in your gross estate. You then transfer cash to your trustee annually to purchase your trust. The gift tax of this transfer can be avoided by including a provision called Crummey power. This provision allows gifts to the trust to qualify for the federal annual gift tax exclusion. Premium payments are made by the trustee/beneficiary. Upon your death, your trustee will receive the insurance policy's death benefits. Now, the trustee has access to making loans to your estate, to buy assets from the estate, and to donate funds to the estate to help pay estate settlement costs.

Many people try to avoid probate because they do not like the idea of all assets becoming public record at death. Beneficiary designations on life insurance, annuities, and retirement accounts can help to avoid probate. Also, some planning techniques, such as setting up a living trust, will allow you to circumvent probate. However, rules regarding living trusts vary by state, so depending on which state you live in the living trust may not be the best alternative.

The Family LLC or LLP

Another alternative planning technique that has become more frequently used over the last several years is a family limited liability partnership. A family limited partnership, or family LLC, is where actual family assets are run like a corporation with both general and limited partners.

For example, this estate planning technique gives the parent who holds the majority of the assets the ability to gift discounted shares of those assets to his heirs. The asset owner can gift more than the normal amount of gifts that are not taxable. Back in 2006, the gift discounted amount

71

was $12,000 per an individual. As a result, he or she can gift out the estate and not have to worry about gift taxes. With a family limited partnership, or LLC, the asset owner or "gift-giver" is alive and gifting parts of the partnership to the kids while the kids do not have any actual control over those gifts. The kids simply receive the shares at a discounted basis which allows the estate owner the ability to maximize the assets of his estate while maintaining control of the assets. This is a very interesting planning technique that you can use in your estate planning.

The AB Trust

In order to take advantage of the applicable tax exemption, there are other techniques to be considered. The AB trust is a living trust with a marital life estate that allows couples to pass the maximum amount of property to their children or other beneficiaries after both spouses die. Each spouse has a will that creates an AB trust.

Another benefit of the AB trust is that it ensures the surviving spouse lives comfortably during his or her lifetime. Instead of leaving property outright to the surviving spouse, generally, each spouse leaves most of his or her property to the trust. Once a spouse dies, the surviving spouse can use the property with certain restriction, but does not own it outright. The property will not be subject to estate tax when the second spouse dies because the second spouse never *legally* owned it.

A drawback of the AB trust, however, is that you have to have an accountant or legal professional to help you with its creation. There will be restrictions on the use of the property. There also will be trust tax returns, which are taxed in the highest tax bracket. It will be important for you to maintain good records.

Charitable Trust

Another technique that can be used for estate planning purposes is a charitable trust. You may consider making a gift of assets and having the charity pay income to you off of those assets. The donation to the charitable trust would give you a tax break. Then, you can use that income from the charity to purchase a life insurance policy. This process is essentially substituting the money in your estate to the life insurance policy, which would then go to your heirs tax free.

When using this technique, however, make sure that you have it set up where you do not actually own the life insurance policy. This is really a general rule that you can use for life insurance policies because if you do own the policy, it will be calculated back into your estate tax. One method to bypass ownership of the policy is to have the life insurance trust on the policy that would pay out to the beneficiaries at your death. Remember, the titling of your assets is crucial to your life insurance policy. Again, do not own your own life insurance policy. You are the insured; the owner should be the life insurance trust.

Estate planning can get quite complicated, expecially when dealing with estate taxes and multiple trusts. Before utilizing any one of these techniques, you should speak to an estate planning attorney.

Chapter 7
Where to look for advice

Many people are eager to offer investment advice. It may be your banker, insurance agent, family member, friend, or even your colleague who offers financial advice. However, if you are seeking legitimate, objective, and trustworthy advice, you should look for a CERTIFIED FINANCIAL PLANNER™ practitioner. Some websites that can help you with your search are www.cfp.net or www.fpa.net. Another network that registers high quality financial advisors is the Paladin Registry, and you can search this registry at www.paladinregistry.com.

Here are some questions to ask a financial professional from whom you are considering as a financial advisor:

Chad Olivier, CFP®

1. What are your credentials and how long have you been in the financial service business?

2. How many clients do you service?

3. How do you handle those clients' assets and problems?

4. What is a typical example of a client?

5. Have you been rated by any services?

6. How do you get paid?

7. How often will you communicate with me?

8. How do you communicate with your clients?

9. What is your philosophy on investing and planning?

10. Why should I choose you as my advisor?

11. Do you have two to three of your clients that are similar to me to call?

As I stated above, ideally you would be asking these questions of a CFP®. Typically, the advisor should have less than 200 clients. This number will enable him or her to give you more personalized attention. If the advisor has more, there should be other qualified staff members that assist the advisor. Is the investor's client base similar to you?

How is the advisor paid - does he or she receive big, upfront commissions without any trailing commissions on assets? Stay away from the big upfront commission. The brokerage industry has pushed that as being good for the client because the internal expenses are lower, but if the advisor does not receive compensation on the performance, there will be less incentive. Make sure you have specifics on how the communication works and the advisor's investment philosophy. Keep in mind: you are looking for someone to help you protect your assets with consistent growth.

Do Not Get Your Financial Advice from the Radio

Like a lot of people, I enjoy listening to talk radio programs, but I often find myself yelling at the radio. Just the other day, a caller called a nationally syndicated show with a host whose main purpose was to give advice on how to get out of debt. What ended up happening was the host tended to go overboard with giving investment advice. Even more aggravating was the fact that this particular host did not have any credentials to give such advice and I cringed every time I heard his attempts; I cannot protect callers from heeding bad advice.

To continue my example, the caller was a 65-year-old man who had just retired and said that his wife wants him to put everything into CDs. Immediately, the host rejected the idea and said "Oh no, don't do that! You can keep your mutual funds and get the 12 to 14%." I was yelling at the radio trying to tell the caller to just hang up. Not only was the host's advice of no value to the man, but the host did not know anything about this retired couple nor did he attempt to find out about their unique situation. In contrast to the host's irrelevant belief, this couple could quite possibly have the majority of their money in CDs and live very comfortably with the security of FDIC insurance. The mutual funds that the host was touting are obviously of much higher risk and one bad year in those types of investments could destroy the newly retired couple's retirement. One bad year could send the retired 65-year-old man back to work. My advice to this host is to stick with telling people to pay off their debt and not try to give investment advice. My advice to you is to not get your financial advice from the radio.

Putting It All Together

This book covered a large amount of information in a relatively simplified fashion. What is so interesting with financial planning is that each one of these individual topics could be a book in itself. Let us look at how to put this information you read into practice. The first thing you need to do is create a detailed list of assets and liabilities. The following should be done:

1. Fund your 3 to 6 months of emergency funds.

2. Calculate your asset protection needs (insurance needs). This should consist of life, disability, car, homeowners, personal liability, and business insurance.

3. Use the investment pyramid to evaluate your current investments and where they fit on your pyramid.

4. Evaluate your current retirement plan and compare it to other plans.

5. Review your will and estate planning documents. Make sure your intentions are listed so that you have the best vehicles to efficiently move those assets out of your estate.

Best of luck with your planning efforts!

Acknowledgements

I would like to thank the following people for helping me with comprising and the many edits for the book: Melody Ritchie, Amy Bercegeay, Ambereen Nasir, Sarah Young, Chris Kuna, and Rose Olivier.

I need to give special thanks to my wife, Rose, who is always the voice of reason with her love, patience, and unselfish sacrifice for the family. I want to thank my two boys, Conrad and Cole, for their bright smiles and sweetness that have enriched my life and put everything in perspective.

I want to thank my Paw Paw Bill even though he passed away when I was just 11 years old. He has had a very big impact on my life. He was a devout family man who constantly wanted his kids and grandkids around. He was a well-respected business man who touched many lives. He died of lung cancer at 54 years old, but has continuously taken care of my grandmother for the past 24 years since his death by providing for her with the insurance and investments in place. It exemplifies his legacy as a true family man – and still my buddy. I still think about you in everything I do, Paw Paw.

I want to thank my dad for showing me how to be my own man. Dad taught me at a very young age that I do not need to go with the crowd. That it was cool to be your own man. Be a leader not a follower. Be honest, and have integrity. This is a man who would rather drink a Coke than a beer, who would travel 10 hour round trip to watch his son play a college tennis match, who would never say a negative word about his wife or kids to anyone, who would give you his word and it meant everything. These are values that I respect and continuously live by his example and will instill in my boys to do the same.

I want to thank my mom for her continuous support and unconditional love. Also, my two sisters Kelli and Colleen and my brother and sister in law Mikee and Gina for allowing me to be the big brother and giving out the big brother advice.

I also would like to thank my clients for giving me the opportunity to help them with their financial planning.